Polluted
Waters

Jennifer Stefanow

Raintree

Chicago, Illinois

First published in North America in 2004 by
Raintree, a division of Reed Elsevier, Inc.
Chicago, Il 60602
Customer Service 888-363-4266
Visit our website at www.raintreelibrary.com

For more information address the publisher:
Raintree, 100 N. LaSalle, Suite 1200, Chicago Il 60602

Printed and bound in Malaysia

08 07 06 05 04
10 9 8 7 6 5 4 3 2 1

© 2004 TIMES MEDIA PRIVATE LIMITED
Series originated and designed by
Times Media Private Limited
A member of the Times Publishing Group
1 New Industrial Road, Singapore 536196

Co-ordinating Editor   : Isabel Thomas
Writer   : Jennifer Stefanow
Series Editor   : Katharine Brown
Project Editor   : Violet Phoon
Series Designer   : Lynn Chin Nyuk Ling
Series Picture Researchers : Thomas Khoo, Joshua Ang

Library of Congress Cataloging-in-Publication Data
Stefanow, Jennifer.
Polluted waters / Jennifer Stefanow.
p. cm. — (Green alert!)
Includes bibliographical references and index.
Contents: Earth's water — Causes and sources — Water pollution and
ecosystem damage — Effects on animals and people — Protection and
conservation — What happens next?
   ISBN 0-7398-7016-5 (library binding – hardcover)
1. Water — Pollution — Juvenile literature. [1. Water — Pollution. 2. Pollution.]
I. Title. II. Series.
   TD422.S74 2004
   363.739'4—dc22   2003019315

The publishers would like to thank the following for permission to reproduce photographs:
• Cover: Photodisc (all) • Title page: AFP • Imprint page: Photodisc, Photodisc, Topham Picturepoint, Hutchison Library (left to right) • AFP: 23 (bottom),
43 (bottom) • Art Directors and Trip Photo Library: 6, 8, 9 (top), 10 (both), 11 (top), 13, 16, 20, 38 (top), 40, 41 • Corbis: 7, 15, 29 (bottom), 36, 37, 44,
45 • Hutchison Library: 22, 31 • Kent State University, Robert Carlson: 11 (bottom) • Lonely Planet Images: 26, 27 (top), 39 • Pietro Scozzari: 17, 25, 33,
42, 43 (top) • Photodisc: 4 (both), 9 (bottom), 12 (both), 14 (bottom), 18, 19 (top), 21 (top), 23 (top), 24, 27 (bottom) • Science Photo Library: 21 (bottom),
28 (top), 38 (bottom) • Still Pictures: 14 (top), 19 (bottom), 29 (top), 30, 32, 34 • Topham Picturepoint: 35 (both), 39

The publishers would like to thank Eric L. Peters, Professor of Ecology and Environmental Science at Chicago State University, for his assistance in the
preparation of this book.

Every effort has been made to contact the copyright holders of any material reproduced in this book. Any omissions will be rectified in subsequent printings
if notice is given to the publishers.

Contents

Words that appear in the glossary are printed in bold, **like this,** the first time they occur in the text.

Earth's Water

Earth is known as the Blue Planet because water covers three-quarters of its surface and makes it look blue from space. Almost all (97 percent) of the water found on Earth is sea water. The **salinity** of the water in oceans and seas makes it unsuitable to drink. Yet more than 275,000 species of sea creatures have already been discovered in our oceans and seas and scientists think that this is where 80 percent of all life on Earth is found. There are also some inland lakes filled with salt water. These include the Great Salt Lake in the United States and the Dead Sea in the Middle East.

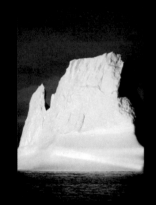

The fresh water that people need to drink makes up only 3 percent of Earth's water. Almost all of this is found underground in the form of ice at the North and South poles. Only 1 percent of fresh water is found at the surface — our rivers, lakes, and **wetlands** are all examples of surface water. Small amounts of water are also found as **water vapor** in the air and clouds. In many countries, people have built artificial lakes, or reservoirs, to collect fresh water that falls as rain.

Three-quarters of the water that is suitable for drinking is stored as ice and snow at the polar regions.

Distribution map showing rainfall minus evaporation.

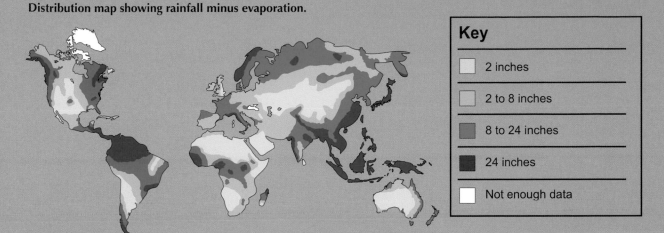

Key

☐	2 inches
☐	2 to 8 inches
■	8 to 24 inches
■	24 inches
☐	Not enough data

Water sources

Fresh water falls as **precipitation** and fills streams, rivers, and lakes. Water that is found above the ground is known as surface water. It is more easily available for people and animals to use than glacial ice or groundwater. Groundwater is fresh water that seeps into the ground and collects in aquifers, the spaces between particles of rock and soil. In some places it also rises to the surface as natural springs. In Saudi Arabia most of the country is covered by desert and this makes finding fresh water a big challenge. So the government has built **desalination** plants to remove the salt from sea water and provide fresh water for people and industries.

How much water do we use?

The amount of water we use is often measured in thousands of gallons per day. 264 gallons will fill about eight bathtubs. The average American household uses about 80 to 100 gallons (300 to 380 liters) a day. But nearly half a billion people in 31 countries, mostly in the Middle East and Africa, do not have enough water. This is because different places in the world do not have the same amount of rainfall. In Africa, rainfall on parts of the west coast can be as much as 80 inches (200 centimeters) per year, while the Sahara Desert in Central Africa has less than 10 inches (25 centimeters) per year. Within the last 100 years, the world population has increased four times and water usage per person has doubled. Soon, more and more people will have to share less and less water.

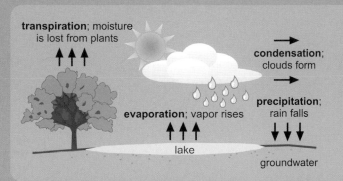

transpiration; moisture is lost from plants

condensation; clouds form

evaporation; vapor rises

precipitation; rain falls

lake

groundwater

The water cycle

Did you know that the amount of water on our planet has remained the same for millions of years? All the water we have in the world is all the water we will ever have. Earth does not lose or gain water. Water is recycled by various processes and is reused over and over again. This movement of water is called the water cycle.

What Is Water Pollution?

Water pollution happens when a **foreign** substance or pollutant, in solid or liquid form, enters water and makes it dirty or unfit to use. The pollutants can come from homes, farms, or factories. Every time we wash our cars or scrub our floors, for example, we create **waste water** that runs off the surface of roads and eventually enters the water sources in our area as **urban runoff.** Water becomes polluted when farms allow animal waste to drain into a river or people dump trash into lakes, rivers, and oceans. Water pollution also occurs when manufacturing plants dump **toxic** chemical waste into rivers.

Pollution enters a river through a sewage outlet that opens into it.

Sources of pollutants

Polluted water is harmful to living things and can make streams, lakes, and coastal waters unpleasant to look at, smell, and swim in. Pollutants can enter our water sources either directly or indirectly. When harmful substances enter a water source directly, it is called point source pollution. An example is when a plastic cup is thrown into a river. When harmful substances enter a water source indirectly, it is called non-point source pollution. This means that the original source or point where the harmful substance entered the water cannot be easily located. One example of non-point source pollution is when vehicle oil washes off roads and into rivers. It is carried to water sources in regions far from the original source.

World Watch Institute, an independent research organization, estimates that 300,000 gallons (1.1 million liters) of sewage are dumped into the Ganges River every minute. The same river provides drinking water for the people.

Water is a precious resource

Water is essential for life so we need to care for our limited water sources. People who live in countries where water is **scarce** have to use the same source of water for drinking, cooking, washing, bathing, and letting farm animals drink. We can increase our clean water supply by taking steps to reduce water pollution. Most countries **treat** their waste water to get rid of bacteria, sediment, and other pollutants. The treated water is then released into rivers and flows into the sea. We can also recycle our water resources. Recycled water can be used by industries, in agriculture to **irrigate** crops, and in homes to wash cars and water yards. The Rouse Hill residential project in Sydney, Australia, expects to supply recycled water from treated waste water to 100,000 homes for nondrinking uses.

Adding to the pollution

Everything we do affects our environment and our supply of safe drinking water because we all live in a **watershed.** All our activities affect the water that passes through our watershed on its way downstream to other watersheds. Any pollution to local water supplies is passed on to other areas and even other countries. Therefore, each area or country depends on the countries upstream to use the water in a responsible way and leave the water clean for others further down the river.

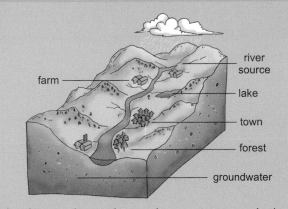

This diagram shows a farm and a town in a watershed.

Forms of Water Pollution

Every day, domestic, agricultural, and industrial activities affect the quality of groundwater and surface water. Agricultural runoff from farms can contain chemicals from pesticides, nitrates from fertilizers, and bacteria from animal waste. These enter rivers, lakes, and oceans. Natural disasters can also lead to water pollution. In 1999, Hurricane Floyd hit North Carolina, a major pig-farming state. Floodwaters carried pig waste, pesticides, fertilizers, and soil into rivers and bays that flowed into the Atlantic Ocean. This polluted the waters of the river mouths, which are important feeding areas for small fish, shrimp, and crabs.

Oil slicks

Spills and leaks from cruise ships, tankers, and oil-drilling projects are a growing problem for marine and coastal wildlife. Ships contribute to ocean pollution when they pump out oily water and wash out their tanks. Oil spreads quickly over large areas of water and is difficult to remove. In November 2002, *The Prestige* tanker was carrying more than 20 million gallons (75 million liters) of oil when it split and sank off the coast of Spain. This created one of the worst environmental disasters in history. Beaches were blackened with thick layers of oil. Thousands of sea birds were contaminated or killed. Oil-stained birds even washed up on the southwestern coast of France.

Oil spills are a visible form of pollution. It can take years to clean up a big oil spill.

Dumping

Because they are so huge, our oceans have become a dumping ground for much of the world's waste. People throw unwanted plastic bags, aluminum cans, and even cars and motorcycles into rivers, seas, and oceans every day. Millions of sea birds, mammals, and turtles suffocate in plastic bags or suffer painful deaths when they get tangled in abandoned fishing nets. Dumping is also carried out by manufacturing plants. These produce between 330 and 550 million tons of **heavy metals, solvents,** toxic sludge, and other waste every year. Industrial waste dumping of heavy metals, such as lead and mercury, poisons our water supply. Pollutants that are dumped onto land often seep into groundwater and contaminate it.

Right: Oil is being held behind a boom in the River Don in Scotland.

Oil in water slowly poisons fish and other marine life.

Agricultural runoff

Fresh water pollution comes mainly from agricultural sources. Land that is poorly drained causes animal waste and fertilizers from farms to run into lakes and rivers. The excess **nutrients** in this runoff can upset the balance of marine and coastal life. They lead to a growth boom of **algae,** which use up the oxygen needed by other plants and animals. Sediment from farm activities can be washed into streams, lakes, or oceans. This smothers coral and seagrass, or covers streambeds in which fish lay their eggs.

Toxic graveyards

When World War II ended in 1945, tens of thousands of bombs filled with chemicals and nerve gas were dumped by U.S., British, and Soviet troops into the Baltic Sea and the eastern Atlantic Ocean. These are now harming the environment. Weapon casings have corroded in the sea water, **leaching** out poisons such as arsenic, mustard gas, and sarin. Strong sea currents move the poisons around and often wash them ashore. Scientists have found that soils in the area contain levels of mustard gas and arsenic that are up to 100 times higher than normal levels. These so-called toxic graveyards are also found in waters off the U.S., Australia, Great Britain, Canada, Japan, and Russia.

Measuring Water Pollution

Polluted water is the world's greatest killer. In developing countries dirty water kills 2.2 million people a year. Most are children. Polluted water transmits diseases such as cholera and typhoid. Exposure to polluted water also causes skin irritation, breathing problems, and poisoning. When scientists take samples of water to test its quality, they look for specific pollutants. We can test water for bacteria, chemicals, heat, and sediment.

Left: An environmental officer collects a sample of water from the River Trent in Great Britain for testing.

Coliform bacteria counts

Coliform bacteria are the most common biological **contaminant.** These are **micro-organisms** that live in large numbers in the intestines of people and animals and help to digest food. When coliform bacteria are detected in water sources, it means that there is human or animal feces in the water. This means that there might be organisms present that can cause water-borne diseases such as cholera, typhoid, and hepatitis. Coliform counts are used to find out the level of coliform bacteria. The process involves counting the number of bacteria in a fixed volume of water.

Right: Water samples are checked for coliform bacteria using a powerful microscope.

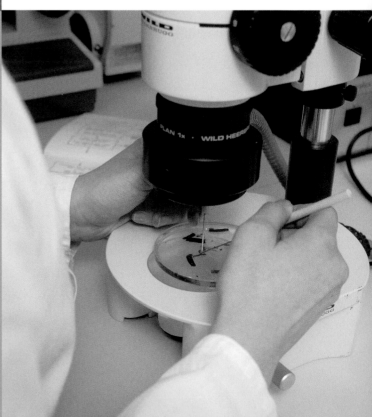

Dissolved oxygen test

Another method of measuring pollution in water is to test for the level of dissolved oxygen. Generally, a higher dissolved oxygen level indicates better water quality. A low dissolved oxygen level means that there is **organic** waste matter in the water being consumed by bacteria, which, in turn, uses up the oxygen in the water.

The amount of organic material, such as food and vegetable waste, in a body of water is measured by the dissolved oxygen test.

Testing for chemical contaminants

Chemicals occur naturally in our water, but high levels of certain chemicals affect our health. Environmental officers test for chemicals in water using the pH (potential of hydrogen) scale. On the pH scale, pure water has a pH level of seven. This is neutral, which means the water is neither **acidic** nor **alkaline.** The lower the pH number, the greater the acidity. The higher the pH number, the greater the alkalinity. Normal water is slightly acidic and has a pH level of about five and a half. Sea water has a pH level of about eight and a half. Pollution, bacterial activity, and water **turbulence** can change the pH levels in water. Acidity in water indicates industrial pollution. Alkaline water is a sign of sewage pollution.

Dye-tests are used to detect nitrates in water. Nitrates are found in fertilizers that enter rivers and lakes as agricultural runoff. Dissolved nitrates in drinking water are harmful to health. The United Nations Global Environment Monitoring System found that nitrate levels were highest in watersheds with intense human activity, such as agriculture. In the U.S., the main source of water pollution is agriculture.

Testing for physical contaminants

Unclear water has many tiny particles, such as silt, suspended in it. These fine particles harm natural **habitats** and reduce visibility in water. An instrument called a Secchi disk is used to measure the physical pollution of water. The disk is painted with black and white segments that become impossible to see when lowered into **turbid** water.

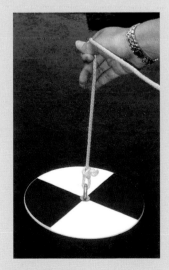

The depth at which the black and white segments of the Secchi disk merge is a measure of the range of visibility in the water.

Glowing fish

Scientists in Singapore are using **gene technology** to develop a type of fish that can detect whether a particular pollutant is present in water. They have introduced red and green **fluorescent** color genes from jellyfish into zebra fish, which are normally black and white. The red and green colors show up well in the presence of chemicals like the female hormone **estrogen** and certain heavy metals. Extra estrogen enters the sewage system and waterways when drugs such as birth control pills are flushed down the toilet. Recent studies in Great Britain suggest that estrogen is the main cause of deformities found in male trout.

Chemical Pollutants

Much of the pollution in water comes from the chemicals used in industry and farming. Chemical pollutants can include mercury, pesticides, and petroleum products. They enter water sources through spills and dumping, or as runoff. For example, the use of some pesticides results in the runoff of arsenic into groundwater. Chemicals enter animal bodies through their mouths, lungs, or skin. These chemicals can build up to high levels in a food chain and become toxic because they do not break down easily. Most chemical pollutants are not visible to the human eye so water that looks clean may contain chemical pollutants.

Heavy metals

Heavy metals like mercury, cadmium, and lead are often deposited with sediment into water sources. They can dissolve in the water and cause metal poisoning when the water is drunk or when seafood that has been in a contaminated environment is eaten. Shellfish such as mussels feed in riverbeds and seabeds and gradually build up high levels of heavy metals and other toxins.

The lead acid in car batteries is a toxic substance that can cause serious health problems when it leaks and is not disposed of properly.

Pesticides

Rain washes away pesticides into streams and rivers as runoff. Some of these chemicals are **biodegradable** and quickly break down into harmless forms. But many are nonbiodegradable and remain toxic for a long time. DDT (dichlorodiphenyltrichloroethane) is a well-known pesticide that is nonbiodegradable. It does not break down into harmless substances over time but builds up in the tissues of animals. Studies performed on the peregrine falcon have shown that DDT causes the falcons' eggshells to become thin. As a result, the eggshells can break easily before they hatch. This has put peregrine falcon populations under threat. DDT use is now banned in many countries.

A sugar cane field is sprayed with pesticides to get rid of insects and other unwanted pests.

Petroleum

Petroleum, or oil, is found under Earth's surface or under the seabed. Petroleum products include gasoline, oil, **lubricants,** and other oil-based products that are used to make plastics and toiletries. These products are a health hazard to people and marine life and poisonous if **ingested.** Benzene, a major component of gasoline, is known to cause cancer in people. Oil can leak from oil refineries, tankers, and industrial waste and cause pollution. Small amounts of oil leak from small boats or jet skis. Oil also seeps naturally into the oceans from beneath the seabed. Natural seepage accounts for 45 percent of the estimated 180 million gallons (680 million liters) of oil released into seas and oceans each year.

Mercury contamination in Minamata Bay

Between 1932 and 1968, a factory producing **acetic acid discharged** liquid waste into Minamata Bay in Japan. The discharge included high concentrations of methyl mercury. Over several years, the fish and shellfish in the bay became contaminated with mercury. People living around the bay who ate the fish and shellfish started to suffer from brain damage, paralysis, and confused speech. It took ten years of **dredging** the bay to remove contaminated sediments.

Biological and Other Pollutants

Many organisms that are present in small numbers in natural water are considered pollutants when found in drinking water. These biological pollutants are microorganisms such as bacteria, viruses, and protozoans or **invertebrates** like worms that cause diseases. *Cryptosporidium parvum* is a parasite that causes diarrhea and stomach cramps in people. The parasite is found in the intestines of cows, deer, and elk. The eggs of the parasites are found in the feces of infected animals. People can get infected if they drink water contaminated with waste material from infected animals.

This turtle is one of the hundreds of sea mammals that get trapped or strangled by abandoned fishing nets each year.

Nonbiodegradable products

Debris such as plastic containers, plastic bags, aluminum cans, glass bottles, fishing nets, and rope is dumped into canals, rivers, and the sea every day. These products remain in the environment without breaking down and float around or get washed up on shores and riverbanks. Plastic bags can choke animals such as sea turtles that mistake them for food. In 2002, volunteers removed more than 4,400 tons of debris from the world's beaches and coastal waters during International Coastal Clean-up Day. The debris included some 675,360 food wrappers and containers, 360,000 aluminum cans, and 14,565 batteries.

Damaged corals are seen at Ningaloo Reef, off the coast of western Australia. Ningaloo Reef is home to more than 200 species of coral and 500 species of fish, many of which are found nowhere else on the planet.

Heat

Manufacturing plants often take water from lakes and rivers to cool electric power plants and return the heated water into the same source. Temperature changes, however small, affect the environment of **aquatic** plants and animals. Warmer water also holds less oxygen and causes aquatic animals to breathe faster to take in more oxygen. Fish and other organisms that are used to the temperature in their environment can die from **thermal** shock.

Sedimentation

Whenever development occurs, for example when we build roads and houses, more sediment enters the surrounding water sources in runoff. The dumping of soil, construction waste, and dredged material into water causes turbidity to increase. Fine soil and sand can clog the gills of fish, and sediment can cover the beds of rivers, streams, and seas and smother marine life such as corals, mussels, and plants.

Ningaloo Reef

Endangered loggerhead turtles, whale sharks, and humpback whales visit Ningaloo Reef, one of the longest coral reefs in the world. In 1997, a proposal to build a coastal marine resort was made. The environmental organization World Wildlife Fund (WWF) warned that this would create environmental problems. Construction would affect water quality. Boats in the area would destroy marine life and introduce marine pests. In July 2003, as a result of protests by the public, the West Australian government rejected the proposal. Ningaloo Reef is now being considered for World Heritage status, which means it would be protected by the United Nations.

Human Causes of Pollution

Population growth increases the demand to feed, clothe, and house people. This demand places pressure on our limited land and water resources. At the same time, human activities in the home, in agriculture, and in manufacturing industries increase the pollution of our water resources. This is why we must act to keep harmful contaminants from entering our watershed and reduce debris by recycling materials and disposing of nonbiodegradable products in a safe way.

Soap and detergents loosen pollutants from car surfaces and roads, then flow into water sources. This is called urban runoff.

Domestic activity

Laundry detergents and nonbiodegradable lawn pesticides and fertilizers are often washed away by rain into drains that are not connected to water treatment plants. The water flows directly into rivers or seas and causes contamination. Litter, vehicle oil spills, and leaks from garages and driveways also get washed into drains. In the 1960s, scientists found that phosphates used in laundry detergents had entered Lake Erie and increased the growth of algae. The oxygen levels in the water fell and fish started to die from **eutrophication.** A law was passed to reduce the use of phosphorus. By 1972, the phosphate content of detergents had been cut by about 90 percent.

In less developed countries, there is a shortage of water. The same water is used for different purposes, making it more polluted each time it is used.

Agricultural activity

Agriculture involves growing crops and raising animals as food for people. Runoff from farms is a growing source of water pollution. Farmers often use large amounts of pesticides, herbicides, and fertilizers to keep pests and weeds away and to encourage crops to grow. Zinc and copper are commonly added to animal feed as nutrients. Livestock such as pigs and cattle produce huge amounts of organic waste. This has to be treated before it is released so that it does not contaminate any groundwater. In Maryland, farmers apply thick layers of manure produced by chicken-rearing farms to fertilize their crops. When it rains, heavy runoff flows into the Pocomoke River and encourages the growth of a toxic algae called *Pfiesteria piscicida* that cause fish to die. A solution was eventually found when the state government helped farmers grow winter wheat crops that reduced soil erosion and runoff.

Industrial activity

Manufacturing industries and thermal power stations contribute to water pollution when they discharge waste water, toxic waste, and chemicals into rivers and oceans without treating them. Some by-products of manufacturing, such as heavy metals, dissolve in water over time. They cause health problems in plants, animals, and people that come into contact with the contaminated water.

The Ganges River

The city of Allahabad in India draws its water from the Ganges River. Millions of people depend on the river for water to drink, cook with, and bathe in. It is respected as a holy site and hundreds of cremations (burning of dead bodies) take place on the banks of the river every day. Animals that use the river as a water source also use it as a toilet. Factories dump chemicals and waste into the river. Agricultural fertilizers and pesticides wash into it from farms up-river. All these have led to the Ganges River becoming greatly polluted.

Natural and Other Causes

The weather and **geology** of an area can contribute to the pollution of its water sources. Winds can carry pollutants to water sources far from their place of origin. Ash from volcanic eruptions and oil leaks from the seabed also pollute water. In 2002, the National Research Council of the U.S. National Academy of Sciences reported that about 180 million gallons (680 million liters) of oil seep from the ocean floor each year. Oil that enters the ocean from human activities account for only 29 million gallons (110 million liters).

Alien species

Alien species are animals or plants that are introduced into new habitats either intentionally or accidentally. Sometimes they do not cause any problems in their new habitats but in many instances they compete with **native species** for food and space. Alien species can be introduced through **ballast water** released by ships or when they take a ride on ship hulls. The cordgrass *Spartina* was introduced to the waters in the English Channel from North America. Cordgrass is a type of marsh plant. It bred with the native species to form common cordgrass and has since spread throughout Great Britain, competing with and replacing native saltmarsh species. *Gymnodinium* was introduced into Australian waters from Japan. This algae causes shellfish poisoning.

Ships take in ballast water at one port and then discharge it at their destination. This can introduce alien species and serious diseases into oceans and seas.

Volcanic eruptions

Erupting volcanoes throw up clouds of toxic chemicals that get washed down to the ground in rain and enter water supplies. Winds also transport these chemicals to wider areas and affect our environment in several ways. For example, sulfur dioxide (SO_2) thrown out by volcanoes returns to the ground in acid rain and poisons lakes. Ash and other debris thrown out by volcanoes can also clog up water sources, increase sedimentation, and upset the balance of marine life.

Other sources

When organic matter decomposes, it pollutes water by releasing extra nutrients into it. Sometimes heavy metals found naturally in soil can be leached out into water sources if there are heavy rains. In Bangladesh, arsenic found naturally in the ground is believed to have leached into thousands of wells. This has led to increased rates of cancer and other illnesses. The arsenic in the wells is found to be as much as 70 times higher than the country's drinking water standard of 0.0000018 ounce per liter.

Zebra mussels

Zebra mussels get their name from the striped pattern on their shells. They are found in eastern Europe and were first discovered in U.S. waters in 1988. They probably arrived in the ballast water of ships that emptied their tanks in the ports of the Great Lakes and have now spread to all the major river systems in the Great Lakes region. They threaten native species because they eat most of the food from the water, effectively starving the native species.

Water Pollution and Ecosystems

Animals feed off plants and, in turn, become food for other animals. This food chain of all animals, plants, bacteria, and fungi in an area, together with their habitats, is called an **ecosystem.** All the members of an ecosystem interact with each other for food and to reproduce. When one part of an ecosystem is damaged or removed, other parts of the ecosystem will be damaged as well.

Damage to coral reefs

Nearly one-third of all fish species live on coral reefs. Coral reefs are formed as generations of coral polyps live, build, and die. Coral polyps are tiny marine animals. They eventually settle on a surface, attach themselves, and build a colony. When they die, they leave behind a hard skeleton. Most reefs today are between 5,000 and 10,000 years old. Tiny algae called zooxanthellae live inside corals and produce oxygen and other nutrients. At the same time, they use the corals' waste products. When higher water temperatures upset reefs, the zooxanthellae leave the corals and the corals are **bleached** white. If the zooxanthellae do not return, the coral polyps cannot produce food and will die. The reef ecosystem depends on the **photosynthesis** that takes place inside corals to produce energy to power the ecosystem. Coral reefs require clear, warm water. They are destroyed by eroded soil that washes into the sea.

Coral reefs grow slowly, at no more than 8 inches (20 centimeters) a year. Removing coral can cause serious damage to reef ecosystems.

Ecosystem damage

Seagrass beds are important feeding areas for turtles and breeding grounds for fish and shrimp. When silt from land reclamation and dredging smothers seagrass beds, habitats are destroyed and the balance of the ecosystem is upset. Oil spills threaten animals and plants in an ecosystem. They block out sunlight that aquatic plants, such as phytoplankton, kelp, and seaweed, need for photosynthesis. Plants die when crude oil coats their surfaces because they cannot absorb energy from sunlight and make food. Marine animals get coated with oil and can no longer swim, feed, and keep warm. Marine birds can no longer fly. Larger animals die of poisoning when they feed on smaller, oil-coated animals.

Left: Activities such as dredging, reclaiming land from the sea, and ships dropping anchors can cause changes in the natural flow of water and affect the habitat of marine animals like this starfish.

Invisible pollutants

Sometimes the pollutants in water are invisible to the naked eye. Even though the water looks clean and clear and all the organisms in it look healthy, pollutants such as bacteria and viruses may be present. Often, these do not harm other organisms in the water. The ecosystem may not be affected until people or animals drink or swim in the water and swallow the **pathogens.** This can lead to poisoning and even death.

Right: Divers collect trash from the seabed.

Food chains

Several food chains make up a food web. There are many food chains in every ecosystem. Food chains pass energy from the Sun along the food chains to all the organisms in the web. Organisms such as grass and algae that can make their own food are known as producers. Organisms that cannot make their own food and need to feed on other plants and animals are known as consumers. **Decomposers** such as fungi and bacteria break down, or decompose, dead organisms and release nutrients, which are then recycled through the ecosystem.

Dead Zone in the Gulf of Mexico

The Gulf of Mexico is located to the south of the U.S. To the west is Mexico and to the east are Cuba and the Caribbean islands. North America's second longest river, the Mississippi River, flows into the Gulf. The Gulf of Mexico supports some of the most productive fish-breeding grounds in the world. Beneath the seabed are huge reservoirs of oil and natural gas.

The Mississippi River Basin

The Mississippi River Basin is the largest basin in North America. The river drains from parts of 31 states before it reaches the Gulf of Mexico. It discharges 494,340 cubic feet (14,000 cubic meters) of water per second into the Gulf. The river is home to a quarter of all fish species in North America and 60 percent of all North American birds use the wetlands in the river basin as part of their migratory flyway. More than 70 million people live in the basin. They raise animals such as cattle and pigs on a large scale. They also farm the land. In fact, the basin is a major producer of corn, soybeans, wheat, cotton, and rice.

At any one time, there are between 3,000 and 5,000 oil and gas rigs extracting oil and gas in the Gulf of Mexico for fuel and to generate electricity.

Dumping in the Gulf

Many people living in the Mississippi River Basin throw household trash into the river. The trash flows into the Gulf and pollutes the water. Fishermen also dump litter out of their boats. The pollution in the water is worsened by oil spills, which occur when oil is transported from the rigs to oil refineries. The main source of pollution, however, is the discharge of fertilizers from farms. These fertilizers carry excess nutrients such as nitrates and phosphates into the Mississippi River, which washes them out into the waters of the Gulf of Mexico.

Cleaning up an oil spill takes a long time and is an expensive process.

A dead zone

The nutrients in agricultural runoff flowing into the Gulf allow algae to bloom. The algae blooms block out sunlight that marine life needs to survive. When the algae die and decompose, the decomposing bacteria use up oxygen in the water. This leaves less oxygen for the plants and animals. Fish and other marine animals are forced to move away. Those that cannot move away die with the plants, leaving a dead or **hypoxic** zone.

There is a dead zone at the mouth of the Mississippi River where it flows into the Gulf of Mexico. The size of this zone varies from year to year and increases in spring when more fertilizers containing trapped nitrates and phosphates are released from melting snow.

The Gulf of Mexico Program

The Gulf of Mexico Program was introduced in 1988 by the Environmental Protection Agency (EPA) to look into the environmental problems in the area. It identifies the main sources of fertilizer runoff and sets down strict guidelines for what farms can and cannot discharge into rivers and streams. The agency also fines people when they throw trash into the water. It has established regulations dealing with oil spills. The Oil Pollution Act of 1990 requires companies with offshore rigs or oil tankers to have a contingency plan in case a spill occurs. It also says that the local authorities have the right to take over an oil-spill clean-up operation if the company's response is not good enough.

Water Pollution and Plants

Plants are almost always found at the start of a food chain. They are the only organisms that can turn sunlight into energy, with the exception of certain bacteria that live in total darkness in the Pacific Ocean. These use chemical energy instead of light energy to make food. If plants are removed from a food chain through water pollution or other means, this major food source for the animals in the food chain will be removed.

When farmers fertilize their crops with rich nutrients, these nutrients often end up in lakes and rivers, causing algae to grow quickly.

Eutrophication

Excess nutrients enter lakes and rivers from agricultural runoff, industrial waste water, and domestic sewage. If there is enough light and water, plants will grow abnormally fast. This increase in the growth of plants is known as eutrophication. Eutrophication clogs water and reduces the amount of oxygen in it. This kills fish and other marine life. Many lakes and rivers in Northern Ireland are rich in nutrients due to the use of phosphorus fertilizers. This has caused algae to grow rapidly in lakes such as Lough Erne and Lough Neagh. Studies show that eutrophication from algae growth is the biggest cause of water pollution in the area. Steps are being taken to reduce phosphorus levels in the water sources. These include removing phosphorus at sewage treatment works in the Lough Neagh catchment area and improving the storage and spread of manure on farms.

Hydrilla grows rapidly into mats that shade and kill other plants in ponds and lakes.

Extinction of native species

The introduction of non-native species is also a form of water pollution. Alien species are a threat to native species because they are usually more **robust** and can grow under difficult environmental conditions. Often, the **predators** that control their growth are not found in the new habitat and their population explodes. Alien plants usually grow fast, need less light, produce many seeds, or have several methods of reproducing. Hydrilla (*Hydrilla verticillata*) was introduced into the United States as an aquarium plant but escaped into the wild. It quickly spread across the U.S. and became an environmental problem. The state of Florida spent $56 million on Hydrilla control over a ten-year period in the 1990s, but the amount of space that Hydrilla occupied in water bodies still doubled. Hydrilla is no longer sold in the U.S.

Acid rain

Acid rain is formed when gases such as sulfur dioxide (SO_2) and nitrogen oxide (NO_2) are released into the atmosphere and react with water vapor in the air to form sulfuric and nitric acid. A body of air can move hundreds of miles in a day and this means that acid rain often falls far away from the source of pollution. Acid rain weakens or destroys forests by leaching essential mineral nutrients such as potassium, calcium, and magnesium from topsoil.

Photosynthesis

Green plants are the only living things that can make their own food. Leaves contain a green pigment called chlorophyll that gives these plants their color. Chlorophyll allows plants to capture solar energy. In a process called photosynthesis, plants use the solar energy to convert carbon dioxide and water into sugars and oxygen. Plants store the sugars in their cells and the oxygen is released into the air, where it is used for respiration.

Shrinking Seagrass Meadows

Seagrasses are flowering plants that grow in shallow waters by the coast and in bays, lagoons, and **estuaries.** They can be found in many tropical areas around the world including Florida, Australia, and the islands of Southeast Asia. Seagrasses are unique because they are the only flowering plants that have adapted to grow in sea water. There are about 60 species of seagrasses worldwide, of which over 30 species can be found in Australian waters. In the last 50 years, about 80 percent of south Australia's seagrass meadows have disappeared from the face of the Earth.

The large seagrass meadows off Victoria, Australia, provide shelter and food for many marine creatures such as this shy dumpling squid.

What are seagrasses?

Seagrasses get their name from having ribbon-like leaf blades. But they are not true grasses. They are more closely related to lilies. Seagrasses have roots and horizontal stems that are buried in sand or mud. These anchor the grasses to the seabed. Seagrasses produce tiny flowers, fruits, and seeds. Currents and tides disperse the seeds and new plants grow where the seeds settle.

A home for marine animals

Seagrass meadows provide a natural habitat for many species of marine animals such as fish, crabs, shrimp, and the unique sea dragon. Fish use the grasses as a nursery for their young. Crabs, shrimp, and sea dragons use the grasses to hide from predators. Seagrasses are also the main source of food for marine animals such as the dugong and the green sea turtle, which swim in the waters off northern Australia. Scientists estimate that an adult dugong eats about 61 pounds (28 kilograms) of seagrass a day while an adult green turtle eats about 4.5 pounds (2 kilograms) a day.

The leafy sea dragon is related to the seahorse. It lives among reeds and seagrass beds in the warm waters around southern and western Australia.

Threats to seagrasses

Researchers at the Pelican Lagoon Research Centre on Kangaroo Island off south Australia estimate that over 15 square miles (40 square kilometers) of seagrasses have been lost since the late 1940s. They believe the loss is caused by increased nutrient levels from urban sewage and agricultural fertilizers that are washed into the water from the mainland. High levels of nitrogen and phosphates have led to excessive growth of seaweeds and algae. These block out sunlight, which the seagrasses need for photosynthesis. The reduction in light affects their growth, eventually killing whole populations. Seagrasses are also being destroyed by other seemingly harmless activities such as boating, jet skiing, and fishing. These activities damage the leaves, stems, and roots of the plants. They also stir up sediment, reducing the level of light in the water. When seagrasses are destroyed, marine animals lose their natural habitat and food source.

Seagrass in Florida

Six species of seagrasses can be found off the coast of Florida and throughout the Caribbean islands. The most common species is turtle grass. The grass blades are flat and grow up to 14 inches (35 centimeters) long and 0.4 inches (1 centimeter) wide. The name refers to the green sea turtles that feed in the area. The second most common seagrass is manatee grass which can grow up to 20 inches (50 centimeters). This species of grass is a favorite food of the manatee (*right*), a large plant-eating marine mammal that lives in the warm waters off Florida.

Water Pollution and Animals

Animals depend on clean water supplies for drinking and living in. Their habitats are seriously damaged when water supplies become polluted. Contaminated water can kill plants and animals. Dumping of trash and oil spills cause the death of thousands of birds and sea animals every year. Aquatic ecosystems often suffer the most from water pollution caused by humans.

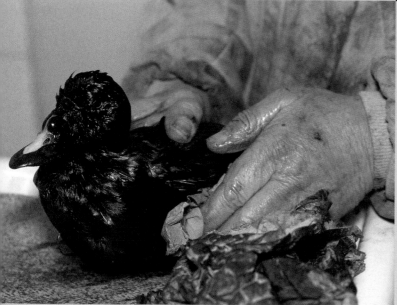

Marine animals are often the victims of human activity. Here, a scorpionfish (top) is caught in a fishing net and a scooter duck (left) is covered in oil after an oil spill.

Mutation

Large numbers of drugs and chemicals are finding their way into the environment. Research shows that estradiol, a drug that replaces estrogen levels in women, causes male fish to grow female organs and produce eggs. Atrazine is a chemical that is widely used in herbicides to control weeds. It is sprayed heavily on crops such as corn and sugar cane. When atrazine is present in agricultural runoff, it contaminates water supplies. Recent studies also show that atrazine upsets the function of normal hormones and causes sexual deformities and death in frogs exposed to it. In frogs, it causes cells to produce the enzyme aromatase and convert the male hormone testosterone into the female hormone estrogen. Atrazine is also thought to be **carcinogenic.**

Fishing nets entangle and harm many seals every year.

Choked to death

When people dump litter on land, rain washes it into drains and canals. It is carried from there into rivers. Trash such as bottles, cans, and plastic containers end up in the sea and pile up in coastal habitats such as mangrove forests, coral reefs, and seagrass beds. Sea turtles often mistake plastic bags for jellyfish and eat them. This blocks their digestive systems and kills them. Fishing lines, nets, and rope can wrap around the fins and flippers of animals and cause them to suffocate. A single nylon mesh net lasts for years and can kill over and over again as trapped animals attract predators that become trapped themselves.

Animal poisoning

Waterfowl, such as swans, geese, and ducks, are often poisoned by discarded fishing tackle (*left*). When these birds eat lead sinkers from fishing lines or lead shot from shooting trips, the heavy metal dissolves in their gizzards and enters their bloodstream. When it reaches toxic levels, it causes paralysis and death. In February 2002, a liquid cyanide spill at a waterhole in the Northern Territory of Australia killed over 400 birds, kangaroos, and other animals. The cyanide was being used to extract gold in a nearby mine. Analysis of the contamination found that the cyanide concentration was 2,000 **parts per million.** This is deadly even for humans.

The *Exxon Valdez Disaster*

The state of Alaska covers 571,400 square miles (1.48 million square kilometers) of land. Prince William Sound along the Alaskan coastline has 3,000 miles (4,830 kilometers) of shoreline. On March 23, 1989, the oil tanker *Exxon Valdez* ran aground on Bligh Reef in Prince William Sound in Alaska. The tanker spilled about 11 million gallons (42 million liters) of oil into the ocean.

Frozen to death

Seals, otters, seabirds, and other animals that lived along the shoreline and coast were immediately coated with layers of oil. Oil injures animals in many ways. It covers their feathers or fur and ruins the ability of their thick coats to keep them warm. The waters of Alaska are very cold and many of the animals affected by the *Exxon Valdez* spill froze to death because of a lack of **insulation.** As the animals tried to clean themselves, they swallowed the oil and were poisoned. Some animals died immediately, while others suffered organ damage or blindness and had a slow and painful death. Those that escaped death often suffered reproductive difficulties later in life.

The Exxon Valdez *pumps the oil that did not spill into the ocean into the* Baton Rouge. *The amount of oil spilled into the sea as a result of the accident would have easily filled 125 Olympic-size swimming pools.*

The clean-up

Various methods were used to clean up the oil spill. Hot water was sprayed using high pressure hoses to break up the oil. Unfortunately, the hot water also killed many animals and plants along the shoreline. In some areas the high pressure from the hose killed wildlife. Chemicals were used to remove the oil but they left some oil behind. Bulldozers and tractors were brought in to remove large deposits of oil-covered sediment washed in by the tide but they could not remove oil floating on the water. Finally, rescue workers tried bioremediation. This is a new process that uses organisms to remove hazardous organic contaminants. A special chemical called Inipol EAP22 was used to encourage the growth of oil-eating bacteria. This quickened the breakdown of oil.

A massive clean-up exercise takes place after an oil spill. After the Exxon Valdez *oil spill, the layer of oil on nearby beaches was about 3 feet (1 meter) thick.*

After the spill

Ten years after the spill, researchers reported that recovering species included the common murres (a black-and-white sea bird that accounted for about three-quarters of the 30,000 dead birds collected in the four months after the spill), clams, mussels, common loons, cormorants, harbor seals, harlequin ducks, and pigeon guillemots. Those that did not show recovery included the population of Prince William Sound killer whales. Only bald eagle and sea otter populations were considered fully recovered after ten years.

The final death toll

No one knows exactly how many animals were killed or injured. More than 35,000 dead birds and 1,000 dead sea otters were found after the spill. But this is thought to be only a small fraction of the actual death toll, since most carcasses sank. Researchers estimate a death toll of 250,000 sea birds, 2,800 sea otters, 300 harbor seals, 250 bald eagles, up to 22 killer whales, and billions of salmon and herring eggs. More than 450 sea otters were rescued after the spill. When the clean-up was over, 197 of these sea otters were released back into the wild. Scientists have since been following their progress.

Water Pollution and People

It is estimated that 1.1 billion people in the world do not have access to safe drinking water. The majority of these, about 900 million people, live in China, India, Indonesia, Pakistan, and Nigeria. People in developed countries use ten times more water than those in less developed countries. The United States uses more water than any other country in the world. Ninety percent of its water is used for industry and agriculture. In less developed countries, the shortage of safe drinking water is made worse by the lack of technology to manage water resources. Poor sanitation adds to the pollution of available water.

Poisoning

Chemical pollutants in water sources can cause diseases in people if consumed. Some of these chemicals accumulate in the body over many years because they do not break down easily and have toxic effects. For example, nitrates from fertilizer runoff can cause blood disorders in people who drink water from polluted wells. Mercury and arsenic poisoning cause deaths if drinking water is severely contaminated.

Trash is dumped near this standpipe where water is collected for washing and drinking.

A 2003 United Nations report says that one person in six has no regular access to safe drinking water. Many of these people also have to use the same water source to wash their clothes.

Diseases

The effect and spread of disease through water is much worse when hygiene standards are low and sanitation facilities are poor. In many less developed countries, it is usual for human and animal waste to be dumped in ditches, canals, and streams without treatment. Diseases carried in polluted water cause the death of about 3 million people a year worldwide. In the early 1990s, untreated sewage water that was used to fertilize vegetable fields caused outbreaks of cholera in Chile and Peru. In Buenos Aires, Argentina, a slum neighborhood faced continual outbreaks of cholera, hepatitis, and meningitis because only 4 percent of homes had a proper water supply or toilets.

Shortage of clean drinking water

The use of fresh water increased more than twice the rate of the world population in the 20th century. As a result, our rivers, lakes, and seas have become increasingly clogged with waste, toxins, and untreated sewage. Pollution makes water unfit to use. More than 2 billion people depend on underground water but **water tables** around the world are dropping by about 10 feet (3 meters) a year across the world, according to a United Nations Environment Programme (UNEP) study. Today, four out of every ten people throughout the world live in countries that do not have enough water.

Water from air

After years of research and development, inventors in the United States have designed a machine that can produce pure drinking water from the surrounding air. Air is passed through the machine which extracts moisture through a process called condensation. The water droplets are collected and filtered through a micro carbon filter to remove very tiny parts and pollutants. The water is then purified in an ultra-violet purification chamber, which eliminates almost 100 percent of the bacteria, viruses, and harmful toxins in it. Large machines can produce several thousand gallons of pure clean drinking water per day, at one-sixth of the cost of bottled water in the U.S. This will give people access to clean water and help them to avoid drinking contaminated surface water and groundwater.

Fallout at Chernobyl

Chernobyl is a town located in Ukraine in eastern Europe, formerly a part of the Soviet Union. It is the site of the world's worst nuclear disaster. On April 26, 1986, an explosion at the Chernobyl nuclear plant released radioactive material into the atmosphere. The amount of radiation that escaped during the disaster was estimated to be 200 times higher than that released from the atom bombs that were dropped on Hiroshima and Nagasaki, Japan, during World War II. Millions of people were exposed to radiation.

Unsafe food and water

In Ukraine and neighboring Belarus and Russia, radioactive particles poisoned lakes, rivers, streams, and groundwater sources. Within days of the accident, many rivers in Ukraine showed high levels of these particles. This caused an immediate shortage of safe drinking water. The rivers, in turn, contaminated the soil as they carried the radioactive particles downstream. Aquatic plants and animals absorbed the radioactive particles in the water. When people ate the plants and animals, they ingested radioactive material as well.

Scientists wearing special protective suits measure the amount of radiation present in the air in an area next to the Chernobyl nuclear power plant.

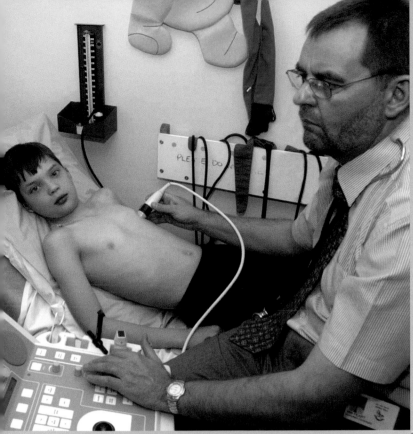

Health problems

One of the radioactive particles released in the fires was strontium-90. In people, radioactive strontium can cause bone tumors and even leukemia, a blood disease in which the body produces too many white blood cells. Strontium-90 and radioactive caseium-137 still contaminate the soils and waters around Chernobyl. Among newborn infants, doctors have noted an increase in the number of babies born with birth defects.

A doctor examines a boy who was exposed to radiation from the Chernobyl nuclear power plant disaster.

Contamination remains

Even though the Chernobyl meltdown happened almost twenty years ago, nearby rivers and lakes remain highly radioactive. These rivers continue to spread radioactive matter further and further away each year. There is heavy snowfall in this cold region. When the snow melts in spring, the rivers flood. Thousands of gallons of water wash over the contaminated soil and spread the radiation in two ways: first by carrying radioactive particles from the soil into another body of water through its watershed; and second by soaking through the contaminated soil into underground water tables and creating huge reserves of poisoned groundwater.

Trees damaged by radiation take on a reddish hue. Radioactive particles in topsoil and roadside dust, ready to be stirred up, are a constant danger.

Cleaning up Chernobyl

In July 2000, 40 nations pledged $370 million to continue cleaning up the area. Since then, the money has been used to repair cracks that have appeared in the concrete casing that enclosed the reactor building. Robots have also been designed to take over some of the cleaning jobs in areas where the radiation level is still high. Scientists are using bioremediation here as well to remove harmful pollutants from contaminated soil or water. Sunflowers, tobacco plant seedlings, and Indian mustard absorb strontium from the soil or water. These plants are then disposed of carefully as radioactive waste.

International Cooperation

The International Coastal Cleanup (ICC) is organized by The Ocean Conservancy, the oldest and largest volunteer organization in the world working for the protection of Earth's oceans. The Ocean Conservancy was founded in Maryland in the 1970s. In 1986, a staff member who was disgusted by the litter she found on Texas beaches started the Texas Coastal Cleanup. By 1989, it had become the International Coastal Cleanup. Since then, over 5.2 million volunteers from 123 countries have participated in the ICC.

Adopt a coastline

The ICC campaigns encourage volunteer groups to adopt a section of their country's coastline and clean it up. The volunteers measure and record the types of pollution and debris found there. In the 17th annual clean-up in 2002, volunteers combed 12,410 miles (19,970 kilometers) of coastline. They collected almost 4,500 tons of trash and found 259 entangled animals worldwide.

Children from a town north of Belgrade, Yugoslavia, hold signs with slogans against the pollution of the River Tisa after a cyanide spill in a Romanian gold mine polluted the waters of the river.

Ocean Wilderness Pledge

People can show local politicians their care and concern for ocean habitats by signing the Ocean Wilderness Pledge, a campaign launched by The Ocean Conservancy. Individuals who sign the pledge agree to preserve ocean wilderness and **conserve** ocean life, from the largest blue whale to the smallest plankton. They do this for their benefit, the benefit of their country, and the benefit of future generations.

A man and his child watch workers clear oil and trash after an oil spill at Newport Beach, California.

Activist Network

The Ocean Conservancy also helps people support ocean conservation through its Activist Network. Members are notified by email when legislation, industrial, or other concerns threaten ocean preservation in their country. Volunteers can then take action by signing petitions to influence business leaders and government officials.

Clean Up the World

Clean Up the World started as an idea by Australian yachtsman Ian Kiernan. As he sailed around the world in his yacht, *Spirit of Sydney*, he was shocked by the pollution that he came across. In the Sargasso Sea south of Bermuda, he saw floating plastic bags, toothpaste tubes, and broken plastic buckets. When he returned to Australia, he launched Clean-Up Sydney Harbor Day in 1989. More than 40,000 people cleaned up the harbor. Tons of rusted car bodies, plastics, glass bottles, and cigarette butts were removed. The success of this event led to the first Clean Up Australia Day in 1990. After twelve years of organizing the event, Kiernan gained the support of the United Nations Environment Programme (UNEP). Clean Up the World was launched in 1993. Today more than 40 million volunteers in 120 countries spend one day a year cleaning up a local area.

Water Shortage in China

China is the fourth largest country in the world after the United States. It is located in eastern Asia. It is the world's most highly populated country, with 1.28 billion people. One problem facing China today is supplying enough clean water to all its citizens. Many of its rivers have dried up. Most of its lakes, reservoirs, canals, and rivers are covered in algae or water hyacinth. Half the watersheds of China's seven main rivers are contaminated by industrial, farm, and domestic waste. Only 25 percent of its 23.1 billion tons of domestic sewage is treated.

Part of the Yangtze River. The Three Gorges Dam being built on the river will control its flow from Wuhan in Hubei province to Chongqing in Sichuan province.

Polluted water

In the 1990s, 80 percent of the surface water available in China was found to be contaminated. Eighty-five percent of groundwater was also polluted from leaking underground industrial storage tanks and the improper disposal of hazardous waste. As a result, 78 percent of China's cities had water supplies below the national drinking water standards, and only 20 percent of China's rivers contained water suitable for agricultural use.

When ready, the Three Gorges Dam will supply water to the 20 million inhabitants in Shanghai, China's largest city.

The largest dam in the world

To meet the water and electricity needs of its ever increasing population, China is constructing the largest dam in the world to contain the world's third largest river, the Yangtze. Over 1 million people will have to be resettled but when completed in 2009, the dam will create a 369-mile (595-kilometer) long lake that will provide clean drinking water and hydroelectricity to Chinese citizens.

Cleaning up three rivers and three lakes

The Chinese government is also cleaning up the waters of the Huaihe, Liaohe, and Haihe rivers and Dianchi, Taihu, and Chaohu lakes. By 2010, the government will have increased the number of water treatment facilities along these rivers and lakes. As a result, the quality of drinking water from these sources is expected to improve and meet national drinking water standards.

Tianjin city

The industrial city of Tianjin on the banks of the Hai River in northeastern China has 9 million people. The tributaries that feed the Hai River are almost dry but waste continues to be dumped on the dry riverbed. In the reservoirs, agricultural runoff from fertilizers and sewage have made the water unsafe for drinking. The water shortage is so bad that the local authority has shut down public baths and rationed water. Hundreds of officials also patrol the river to prevent water from being taken.

The East Kolkata Wetlands

Kolkata (Calcutta) is the capital city of the state of West Bengal in India. It is one of the most highly populated urban cities in the world with approximately 11 million inhabitants. The climate is hot and humid with monsoon rains that fall mainly from mid-June to mid-October. Annual average rainfall is 63 inches (1,600 millimeters). January is the coolest month and May the hottest. The region is part of the River Ganges **delta.** Over the years, sediment deposits have moved the course of the river and many of its streams have dried up.

Dried ponds

The wetlands to the east of Kolkata have been used as **brackish-water** fish farms since the late 1800s. The area receives water from the Bay of Bengal through the Bidyadhari River. Most of the people in the wetlands grow vegetables on small plots as a household activity and raise fish for a living. In 1928, sediment build-up on the delta of the Bay caused the Bidyadhari River to dry up and the water supply to the wetlands and fish farms stopped.

Children play in the dried up Bay of Bengal.

The waste water-fed ponds in the East Kolkata Wetlands produce about 14,300 tons of fish annually.

Sewage for fish

A fish farmer found that domestic sewage water from surrounding towns could form another source of water for the farms. Sewage water was allowed to sit in the fish ponds before fish were introduced. This gave the bacteria in the water an opportunity to decompose the organic matter in the sewage. At the same time, this removed sewage from the water. Algae found in the ponds also provided food for the fish.

Success

Today, the East Kolkata Wetlands support almost 300 fish ponds and cover an area of about 13.5 square miles (35 square kilometers). There are at least three towns in Kolkata whose waste water is treated and reused in ponds managed entirely by villagers. This saves them enough money to pay for the cost of pumping waste water into the ponds. Excess water is released into rice fields or used to irrigate vegetable farms.

Bacterial digestion

Bacterial digestion is the process of bacteria consuming organic matter. The bacteria feed on the organic waste and get nutrition for growth and reproduction. The organic waste is broken down into water and carbon dioxide by complex chemical reactions. This removes odors and pollutants from organic waste.

Global Citizens

Water pollution is a global problem. It affects the health of all life on Earth and water cleanliness should be the concern of all. Watersheds have no boundaries and pollution that occurs in the waterways of one country can affect millions of people downstream in other countries. Many governments, organizations, and individuals are working towards providing better quality water worldwide. International treaties have been signed to control water pollution. For example, the North Sea countries have agreed to stop dumping sewage and industrial matter, burning toxic waste, and to reduce river pollution.

Clean Water Act in the United States

The Clean Water Act of 1972 is concerned with the quality of surface water in the U.S. It attempts to reduce direct pollutant discharges into waterways and treatment facilities, and to manage polluted runoff. Its goal is to restore and maintain the chemical, physical, and biological cleanliness of the nation's waters so that they can support fish, shellfish, wildlife, and human recreation in and on the water. First, the focus was on chemical, biological, and physical causes of water pollution. Now, it focuses on managing watersheds as a whole rather than as individual areas.

Citizens of the Philippines receive water distributed by their government because drinking water is scarce in areas of the country.

Vision 21

The Water Supply and Sanitation Collaborative Council is an international organization concerned with water supply and sanitation for people in less developed countries worldwide. It estimates that a person needs 2.6 to 4 gallons (10 to 15 liters) of clean water a day for personal needs such as drinking and cooking. Unfortunately, today about 1.1 billion people do not have safe drinking water. Vision 21 is a movement started by the Council to put an end to a global crisis. Its mission is to have 'A Clean and Healthy World: A world in which every person has safe and adequate water and sanitation and lives in a hygienic environment.' It aims to do this by 2025.

Nigerian children wash their faces using water from a tap installed in their village. Many African countries, including Nigeria, face serious water shortages.

World Bank

International agencies like the World Bank loan money to developing countries to clean up polluted water. China received a loan of $150 million in 2000. It will use this to control the pollution of water sources from industrial waste water in cities in the Hebei province. The province will provide $140 million for the cities of Shijiazhuang, Handan, and Tangshan to reduce water pollution and increase the supply of clean water. The World Bank currently funds 21 individual water source-related projects with total loans of $807 million.

A group of Chinese women wash their laundry in a roadside drain. Pollution of water sources is a serious problem in China.

In a nutshell

Water pollution is caused by: • human activities such as spills and dumping • sedimentation • urban and agricultural runoff • introduction of new species • industrial pollutants and sewage • natural disasters such as volcanic eruptions • acid rain

Water pollution results in: • shortage of clean water for drinking, cooking, and for agriculture • illness and death • destruction of ecosystems • loss of biological diversity

What Can I Do?

Clean water is essential to all life on land and in the oceans. Our water sources are limited. If we pollute them, there is less water for everyone to share. We can do our part to preserve our environment and keep our water safe from further pollution. Help conserve our environment! Here are some ways you can help.

Clean it up!

- Organize a 'clean-up-the-beach or riverbank' day at a water source near your school and see how much trash you and your class pick up.

- Select a local beach or riverbank to clean. Low tide may be the best time to find trash left on the shoreline. Make sure an adult is present whenever you work or play near water.

- You will need thick rubber gloves, bags for trash, tongs to pick up debris, sunscreen and a hat for protection from the sun, water to drink, and a notebook.

- At the chosen site, pick up with tongs all the trash that you find. Do not use your bare hands to pick anything up. Ask an adult or teacher for assistance if you find a dead animal or chemical waste containers.

- Sort out all the trash at the end of the day and fill in the total number of each item in your notebook under these headings: plastic, paper, metal, cloth, glass, wood.

A child collects trash from a beach as part of a clean-up-a-beach campaign.

Study a mini-water cycle

Set up an enclosed ecosystem to observe the water cycle. You will need a glass tank or large glass jar and a cover that can be tightly sealed. You will also need a watering can, soil, sand, pebbles, small rocks, and small plants such as moss and ferns.

- Wash the glass container and put a layer of soil, pebbles, and sand on the bottom of the container.
- Arrange the plants in the container and water them well.
- Seal the container and keep it in a well-lit spot but not in direct sunlight.
- Observe how water evaporates and condenses on the sides of the jar or is taken up by plants and released by evaporation. The plants will not need extra water for a long time. All the water you put in when you first watered the plants is all that is needed. It is reused again and again.

Conduct a water quality test

Is the water in your area clean? Does it contain fertilizers from runoff? This simple water quality test will help you to find out. Visit a local water source such as a pond or stream. Measure its water quality by taking readings of pH, temperature, dissolved oxygen, and nitrate and phosphate levels. Always make sure an adult is present whenever you work or play near water.

- Ask if your school science laboratory has a water quality testing kit that you can borrow. A simple kit may also be bought from a pet shop.
- Choose a local water source with the help of a teacher or another adult.
- Carry out the tests with samples taken from the water. Water samples must all be taken at the same spot and at the same time for readings to be accurate. Record the data in the table below and compare the readings with the scales given in the test kit.
- You could compare readings taken from the source at different times of the day or year to see if there are any differences. (For example, nitrate levels may change according to season. In spring, when ice containing nitrates starts to melt, the levels of these chemicals in streams and rivers will increase.)

WATER QUALITY TEST RESULTS	Location 1 Time:	Location 2 Time:	Location 3 Time:	Location 4 Time:
pH				
Temperature				
Dissolved oxygen level				
Nitrate or Nitrogen level				
Phosphate or Phosphorus level				

Glossary

acetic acid colorless acid with a strong smell, as in vinegar

acidic substance with a sour taste and a pH level that is lower than seven. Strong acids can dissolve even metal.

algae small plant such as seaweed that grows in or near water and does not have ordinary leaves or roots

alkaline having a pH level greater than seven. Alkaline substances often have a soapy feel and a bitter taste.

aquatic ability to live in or on water

ballast water water or other heavy matter used at the bottom of a ship to make it heavier

biodegradable able to decay naturally and harmlessly

bleach remove color from a substance

brackish-water combination of salt water and fresh water

carcinogenic that can cause cancer

condense change from gas to liquid or solid form as a result of becoming cool

conserve protect from harm and prevent wasteful use of resources

contaminant something that makes a substance impure by mixing it with something unclean or bad

decomposer fungus or bacterium that breaks down dead organisms and releases nutrients

delta area of low, flat land where a river splits and spreads out into several branches before entering the sea

desalination process of removing salt from seawater

discharge send out

dredge remove unwanted objects from a river or lake

ecosystem community of plants and animals in a physical environment

estrogen chemical substance produced in the body that causes change in reproductive organs

estuary river mouth

eutrophication process in which a water source becomes so rich in nutrients that there is an overgrowth of algae, and natural wildlife is unable to survive

evaporate change from liquid to gas by heating

fluorescent having a very bright or glowing appearance

foreign belonging to another place

gene technology scientific method that uses information about DNA to change life forms

geology study of Earth's structure, surface, and origins

habitat natural home of an animal or a plant

heavy metal metallic substance that is harmful to our health

hypoxic not having enough oxygen

ingest take into the stomach; eat

insulation substance which prevents heat from escaping

invertebrate animal without a backbone

irrigate supply water to agricultural land by artificial means

leaching process by which soluble materials, such as salts and nutrients, are washed away into water

lubricant grease or oil

microorganism very small living thing which can only be seen under a microscope

native species plant or animal that grows naturally in a place

nutrient substance required by a living thing for growth and energy. Plants need carbon dioxide and water, as well as nitrogen and magnesium, which can often be obtained from the soil.

organic made of living things such as plants and animals

parts per million number of parts of a substance found in one million parts of a particular gas, liquid, or solid

pathogen bacterium or virus that can cause a disease

photosynthesize use light energy to make food from carbon dioxide and water. Only green plants photosynthesize because they have chlorophyll.

precipitation water that falls to Earth as rain, snow, sleet, or hail

predator animal that hunts and kills other animals

robust strong and healthy

runoff water that flows across the surface of the ground

salinity amount of salt in a body of water

scarce not easy to find

solvent liquid that dissolves solids

thermal power energy based on heat

toxic containing poison

transpire lose moisture from the surface

treat apply special substances to give a particular quality

turbid substance that is not clear because a lot of small particles are in it

turbulence strong movements in air or water

urban related to a city or town

waste water any water resulting from runoff, industrial waste, agricultural waste or human sewage that is not safe for use

water vapor water in the form of a gas

watershed area that drains to a common waterway; a river, stream

water table level below the surface of the ground at which water is found

wetland area where water covers the soil or is near the surface of the soil for most of the year

Further Reading

Books:

Dalgleish, Sharon. *Saving Water.* Broomall, Penn.: Chelsea House, 2003.

Hook, Cheryl. *Coral Reefs.* Broomall, Penn.: Chelsea House, 2001.

Mallory, Kenneth. *A Home by the Sea: Protecting Coastal Wildlife.* Collingdale, Penn.: Diane Publishing, 2003.

Markle, Sandra. *After the Oil Spill: The* Exxon Valdez *Disaster, Then and Now.* New York: Walker and Company, 1999.

Nadeau, Isaac. *Water in the Atmosphere.* New York: Rosen Publishing, 2003.

Trueit, Trudi Strain. *The Water Cycle.* Danbury, Conn.: Scholastic Library, 2002.

Videos:

Clean Water. The Earth at Risk series, Schlessinger Media (1993)

The Water Cycle. Earth Science in Action series, Schlessinger Media (2000)

Water Analysis. Science Lab Investigations series, Schlessinger Media (2002)

Water Conservation. Earth Aid series, V.I.E.W Video (1993)

Websites:

Environment Agency – Water
http://www.environment-agency.gov.uk/kids

Marine Pollution
http://home2.pacific.net.sg/~oryanx/index.html

Sydney Water
http://www.sydneywater.com.au/everydropcounts/

U.S. Environmental Protection Agency (Environmental Explorers' Club)
http://www.epa.gov/kids/water.htm

U.S. Geological Survey's Water Science for Schools
http://wwwga.usgs.gov/edu/index.html

Organizations:

Environment Agency
Rio House, Waterside Drive
Aztec West
Almondsbury
Bristol B512 4UD, United Kingdom
Phone: 01454 624400
Fax: 01454 624409
http://www.environment-agency.gov.uk/

Environmental Protection Agency
40 City Road
Southbank
Victoria 3006,
Australia
Phone: 03 9695 2722
Fax: 03 9695 2785
http://www.epa.vic.gov.au

Greenpeace USA
702 H Street NW, Suite 300
Washington DC 20001
Phone: 202 462 1177
Fax: 202 462 4507
http://www.greenpeaceusa.org

World Wide Fund for Nature
WWF-UK
Panda House, Weyside Park
Godalming, Surrey GU7 1XR
United Kingdom
Phone: 1483 426 444; 1483 426 408
http://www.wwf-uk.org

Disclaimer: All the Internet addresses (URLs) given in this book were valid at the time of going to press. However, due to the dynamic nature of the Internet, some addresses may have changed or sites may have changed or ceased to exist since publication. While the author and Publisher regret any inconvenience this may cause readers, no responsibility for any such changes can be accepted by either the author or the Publisher.

Index